# The Faith Promise Concept

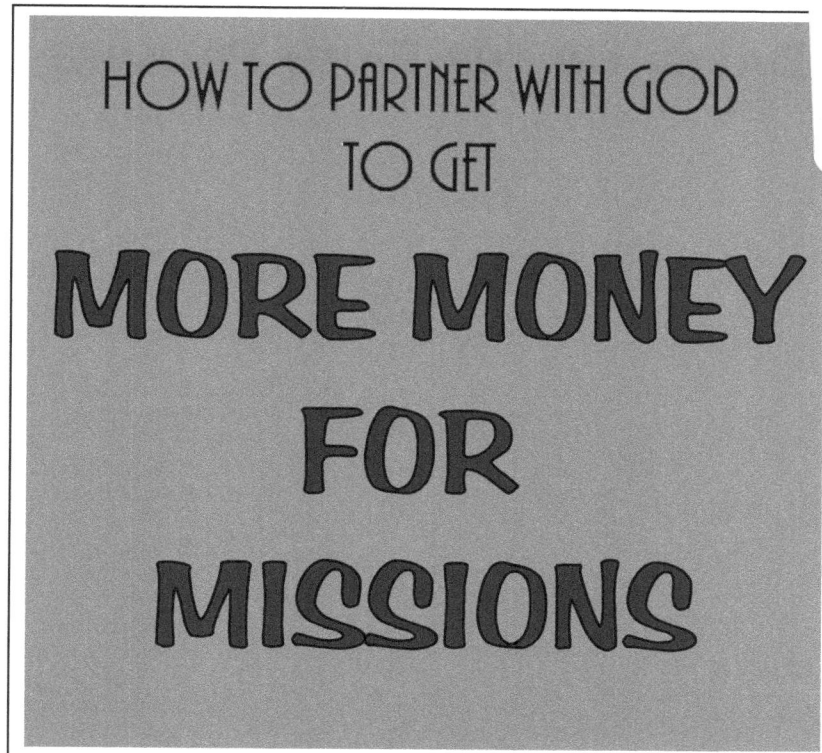

HOW TO PARTNER WITH GOD
TO GET

# MORE MONEY
# FOR
# MISSIONS

BY
GUY BONGIOVANNI, D. MIN.

A companion DVD Version of this Manual is available at
FaithPromise@zoominternet.net .
It includes in downloadable and printable format all the pages
in this Manual PLUS the audio-visual presentation
on the Faith Promise Concept.

House
Of
Bon
Giovanni
PUBLISHERS OF GOOD NEWS

**Division of Life Enrichment Ministries, Inc.**
EMAIL: FaithPromise@zoominternet.net

# A MANUAL OF RESOURCES
# FOR DEVELOPING A MISSIONS CONVENTION
# BASED ON THE FAITH PROMISE

First printing 2014
Printed in the United States of America

**ISBN 978-0-912981-34-5**

# Preface

Some would call it coincidence. I prefer, Providence.

The phone call that afternoon from Dale Russo, Executive Director of Missions for the International Fellowship of Christian Assemblies was uncanny. He wanted to know if I would be interested in collaborating with him in producing a DVD about the Faith Promise concept! What made it uncanny was that earlier that morning, while looking through my files for another item, my eyes fell upon my Faith Promise file. I picked it up and leafed through the contents with nostalgic memories until my eyes came upon the "story board" on the Faith Promise I had developed years earlier. I intended someday to produce a Power Point to help Pastors implement the Faith Promise during their Missions Conventions. As I quickly looked over it again, the thought crossed my mind: someday I really need to get this done.

Clearly, Dale's call was more than casual. I assured Dale of my interest; that I even had the text already written for the narration. And as it's said, "The rest is history." I put together a Power Point. Dale engaged Tim Tyler, who before his pastoral ministry worked as an artist for General Motors in Detroit, Michigan. He put it all together with beautiful Graphics. And with the encouragement of Michael Player, General Overseer of the IFCA, the project moved forward. I added a MENU of resources as a further help to our colleagues and the DVD is now complete.

My passion in producing this DVD is that it might help our colleagues focus sharply upon the major underlying idea of the Faith Promise. Too many presentations miss the mark! Stressing the power of faith, world need, even how we can help with our money, won't do it! Even if Faith Promise terminology is used, without clearly explaining what a Faith Promise is, it falls short. It's confusing, denies the people opportunity to give from a higher motivation and jeopardizes maximum receipts for mission. It's indispensible that every individual gets his personal word of direction from the Lord; and that he promises to trust God to supply it, by a miracle if necessary. One must sense he has been commissioned by the Lord to trust Him to supply a specific amount of money for Missions through him. That's the very heart of the Faith Promise - the key that releases monies for missions! If we miss this, we've missed the very heart of it and cripple our potential. Leadership must focus sharply on this idea and cultivate it aggressively and intentionally.

If we waver in our leadership in missions; if we waffle in our focus on the unreached; if we misconstrue "passing the plate" as giving to missions; if we interchange references to missions giving as a pledge, a faith pledge or a faith promise, we risk hopelessly confusing our congregations and makes activating a genuine Faith Promise extremely difficult. This is counterproductive. The Faith Promise is crippled by uncertainty and instability. In a productive environment for missions, missions should be priority, "pledge" should be a "bad word" and faith in God's supply should be the pervasive climate. I hope this DVD will be both inspirational and instructive.

~Guy BonGiovanni, D. Min.

Canfield, OH
October 19, 2013

# Introduction

Dr. Carl F. H. Henry penned some of the most provocative words ever written. He wrote, "The Gospel is Good News only if it gets there in time!" Take a moment to consider the ramifications of those piercing words. Think of it:

► over two billion individuals (2,000,000,000) never have had the Good News of Jesus presented to them in any format – not even once!

► Five (5) out of every six (6) people die in their sins.

► The worldwide natural birth rate is one hundred thirty five million (135,000,000) per year compared with four million (4,000,000) who accept Christ per year!

► Six thousand eight hundred (6,800) languages have no access to the Bible, not even a single page of the Bible translated into their language.

What is seventy-five thousand (75,000) miles long, wrapping around the earth thirty (30) times and growing twenty (20) miles every day? It is the line of people who do not know Jesus as their Savior. Apparently, after two thousand (2,000) years and with all the advances in technology, the Gospel is *not* getting where it needs to go in time for it to be *Good* News?

A major solution embraces what one of my mentors suggests when he says, "Ministry takes money!" It's a fundamental element. Without finances, the Gospel cannot get where it needs to go, let alone getting there *on time!*

But, "the sky is not falling!" The bright spot in this scenario is that the Lord of Harvest has given us a powerful tool. Through the Faith Promise Concept, our Heavenly Father will provide "money you don't have from sources you don't know about! "

In this DVD and Manual, Rev. Guy BonGiovanni, clearly presents the Faith Promise. The church I serve as Pastor has been witness to the profound impact of this concept. Not only have our church finances stabilized during this recession, but our overall income has risen annually as other churches lost income. Additionally, we sent short term workers to twenty four (24) different countries. Our local outreaches also prospered. And for me, personally, participation in the Faith Promise has opened unique ministries locally and abroad.

Rev. BonGiovanni's presentations on the Faith Promise Concept and his lifetime of "Excellence in Ministry" have been a great inspiration to me; especially in my role as Missions Overseer for the International Fellowship of Christian Assemblies. In fact, his tenure, as one of my predecessors as Director of Missions, has been the standard against which I have measured my own leadership. He has had an awesome impact on my life, the church I pastor, the International Fellowship of Christian Assemblies and missions in general. You might be challenged by the Faith Promise Concept presented in this DVD and Manual; but the rewards are "out of this world." They are eternal!

*Rev. Dale Russo*

**Executive Director of Missions**
**International Fellowship of Christian Assemblies**
**Beaver Falls, PA**

# MENU

# The Faith Promise Concept...

# Learn It !

1. Get a Personal word FROM God

2. Give your word TO God

3. ACTIVELY TRUST God to supply it

4. LOOK for it

5. GIVE it !

# FAITH PROMISE DVD

## Guidelines
## for
## Teachers and Group Leaders

**Verbalizing the concept will
go a long way in helping
people "internalize" it.**

# Guidelines
# for
# Teachers and Small Group Leaders

Allow time for discussion after viewing the DVD. Get your group to talk about what they have just viewed. Discussion will help them process the Faith Promise concept so that it becomes a part of them. Use the following questions to prompt participation. Don't be afraid of repetition. It not only anchors the truth in your group; it also helps the assimilation process which will bring them to a place where the Lord can use them as partners in giving for missions.

## After viewing the DVD:

## Step #1   Lead your Group in Reciting aloud in unison.
"God can provide for missions, money you don't have
from sources you don't know about."

## Step #2  Present the following Questions for answers, clarification and  discussion.
To "break-the-ice" lead off by asking the general question: What is your overall impression of the DVD?  But don't linger on it too long. Then ask the following:

1. **What is the gift God already put in each of us that makes it possible to give to missions regardless of our regular income?**
   -The Diamond of Faith

2. **Tell us what one absolutely needs to have before a Faith Promise can be written; and why it is important.**
   -A word from the Lord
   -It holds us steady when our Faith Promise is tested.

3. **Explain how one gets a word from God on the amount of one's Faith Promise.**
   -Must "hear" the voice of God

4. **What do we mean when we say God _speaks_ to us?**
   -How does God speak?
   -Discuss in what forms the voice of God comes to us

5. **What are some "Ideas for Income" God     might give to generate money for one's Faith Promise?**
   -What are the examples in the DVD?

6. **What should one do once one discovers how much the Lord is leading him to give for missions?**
   -Record it on a Faith Promise.
   -Emphasize this is how we give our word to God!

7. **In what ways might one experience a "trial of his faith" when one registers a Faith Promise?**
   -Money doesn't come in.
   -When it does come in, tempted to use it for other things.

8. **Give a step-by-step procedure for partnering with God in missions with a Faith Promise.**
   1. Get a word from God:  That's God's word to you.
   2. Register a Faith Promise:  That's Your word to God
   3. Trust Him to supply & look for His provision, even from unknown sources or for "Ideas for Income" which you will work, or wisdom & grace to reduce your expense budget.
   4. Give it as it comes in. Read the labels right!

**STEP # 3:** Distribute a Faith Promise card to each person to take home and bring before the Lord for His direction, including being open to ideas the Lord might give him. Urge them to _give the Lord opportunity_ to use them.

**_Close with Prayer._**
Let your group speak freely, but make sure you have enough time to ask each of the questions. This review will help anchor the Faith Promise concept solidly in their minds

----------------------

*"Why should anyone hear the Gospel twice*
*when so many have not heard it once?"*
Oswald J. Smith

# The Faith Promise Concept...

# Think It !

1.  Get a Personal word FROM God

2.  Give your word TO God

3.  ACTIVELY TRUST God to supply it

4.  LOOK for it

5.  GIVE it !

# A Pastor's First Concerns

**If the Pastor doesn't "get it;"
It's doubtful anybody's "got it."**

# 1. Fundamental Decisions

It will spare a Pastor and his helpers a lot of anxiety and confusion if the Pastor immediately thinks-through and makes a determination on the following issues:

1.   **TERMS:**   Will you choose to use *Faith Promise* or *Pledge* in reference to giving?  You shouldn't use both!  Your decision will do much to determine how your people will give. Understand that a Pledge is usually collectable by law, carries that connotation to most folks and can be a big deterrent to commitments of money for anything, including missions.  A Faith Promise is based upon the fruitfulness of one's faith –a different level of giving – based upon what one believes the Lord has directed him to commit and which he promises to give as the Lord provides it.  Using the terms interchangeably is confusing and distracts from the faith perspective of one's commitment. If one decides on using "pledge" to describe what your convention is all about, it actually aborts the heart of a Faith Promise Convention, making much of the data on this DVD irrelevant to what you are doing.

2.   **FREQUENCY:**   Will your Faith Promises be registered again in six months or in one year? Churches do it both ways.  The rationale for a six month registration is difficult for me to understand – if there is one.  Our suggestion is that a church should have an annual Convention and registration. Conventions, if done correctly, are labor intensive.  Having one annually reduces the challenge of enlisting sufficient volunteers for setting up props, displays and a myriad of other tasks to make the time meaningful.

3.   **CONSISTENCY:**   Should we have a Convention as a one-time or as an annual event?  Of course your church will benefit from a one-time event.  But the real benefits to your church come from repeating it year-after-year.  You build on your experience, tweeting the event as needed.  It takes work – lots of it, time and patience.  But an annual Convention pays off.  Your people and Missions purse grow with Convention consistency!

4.   **DESIGNATED OR UNDESIGNATIED:**   Should Faith Promises be designated to specific missionaries,  or is it best to register them Undesignated?  If you lead your people into designated giving, the potential exists that  the more flamboyant, charismatic missionary will draw the larger share of the money and a more retiring, but equally effective –and sometimes a more crucial ministry – will draw less commitments.  Leading your folks into Undesignated giving will permit you and your Missions Committee to make sure distribution of Missions funds is done equitably, balancing all the issues including distribution at Home as well as Abroad.

5.   **BASIC OR COMPLETE:**   Will you lead your people into a Convention with a "Bare-Bones" Convention or one that includes the "tools" that provide special incentives used by the Holy Spirit to maximize their giving?.   You can increase Missions giving just by teaching the Faith Promise concept and give opportunity to register Faith Promises.  But to *maximize the potential* of your people you need to arrange for appropriate visuals, displays, etcs.  Of course, more effort and time are required for this. So, you must determine if the value is worth the additional involvement.  A Complete rather than a Basic Convention is usually more inspirational and productive.

# 2. Getting Started

A. Do the early "Spade Work." Engage your principal Board/Committee in casual to intense discussion and prayer.

<u>Talk and Pray:</u>
1. **About Missions in general**
2. **About Missions as a "coin"**
   a. **Side One: Home Missions** (everything at "Home." Ministries like Teen Challenge, Rescue Missions, Food Ministries, Radio-TV-Online, Convention expenses, etcs.

   *"The light that shines brightest at home, shines furthest abroad"*

   b. **Side Two: Foreign Missions** (everything "Abroad." Support of American and Natiional missionaries, including short-term missions teams, projects, buildings, crusades, literature)

   *"Why should anyone hear the Gospel twice, when so many have not heard it once?"~Oswald J. Smith*

3. **Finding a Balance**
   **IDEAS:**
   a. <u>Use a % of local tithes/offerings for Home Missions</u>
      (Consider impact of your local budget; especially if you have heavy mortgage obligations, etcs.)
   b. <u>Adopt a Progressive Plan</u>: i.e. Begin with a 50-50 Distribution Plan (50% to Home & 50% to Foreign Missions. Then *progressively increase percentages* to Foreign Missions at a rate of 5-10% annually.

|        | HOME | FOREIGN |
|--------|------|---------|
| Year 1 | 50%  | 50%     |
| Year 2 | 40%  | 60%     |
| Year 3 | 30%  | 70%     |
| Year 4 | 20%  | 80%     |
| Year 5 | 10%  | 90%     |
| Year 6 | 0%   | 100%    |

## B. Basic Directives

1.  **You must understand & believe the Faith Promise Concept** and convey it to your people; especially leaders.   Your efforts will be productive in proportion to your convictions.

2.  **You must learn and use the vocabulary of faith**. Words are Powerful.
    The word "pledge" or variation thereof neutralizes the power of the Faith Promise, Confuses Users, and ultimately deteriorates to traditional missions giving.

3. **If you adopt the Faith Promise Concept**, you will need to make two (2) commitments:
    a. <u>You will avoid taking additional offerings</u> – except for emergencies. If your denomination sponsors special missions days –i.e. :Speed the Light….Light for the Lost" etcs, you can adjust your "no additional offerings" policy either by pre-advising your congregation of these "special offerings" as exceptions to your rule, or simply draw from your missions fund an estimated "equivalency" amount and send it as the church's special offering.
    b. <u>You will NOT  collect the money through coercion of any kind.</u>
        (When money doesn't come in, just assure them of your prayers.)

4.  **Saturation is the Key!**  Your congregation should begin hearing about the Faith Promise specifically in all departments at least three (3) Sundays before Ingathering Sunday. And a letter with a Faith Promise card should be mailed to reach each home during the week prior to Ingathering Sunday.

5.  **Appoint a Missions Committee**. You can't do this alone! Include a Board Member, a man,  woman and one young person.  These must be responsible people with a heart for missions. They will work with you in designing and developing your missions convention    as well as determine whom you should support with missions monies. Church Board will,   of course, ratify your support roster. Some of the things you will consider as a Committee:
    a.    A missions banquet with international foods
    b.    Having a display of flags from various countries
    c.    A Parade of Flags during services
    d.    Ushers wearing clothes typical of foreign countries
    e.    A "Thermometer" to track giving as Faith Promises are read
    f.    Missions Displays throughout the church

6.  **Assign a person to each event** agreed upon & a report-back date.

7.  **Appoint a Decorating/Art committee** to create a missions atmosphere throughout the church. Banners usually are available through denominational mission headquarters.

8.  **Draft a Calendar of Events to track progress.**

9.  **Select & contact Missions Speakers & select missions oriented videos.**

10. **Contact Field People in advance** if you want them to participate via video, Skype, etc.

11. **Keep the Focus of the People on Two (2) facts**:
    a. *Objective*: Individuals must get a word from the Lord *for themselves* re: how much to give;
    b. *The church will reveal where it's "Faith Level" is for missions* by the TOTAL Faith Promises the congregation registers on Ingathering Sunday.

12. **Train your Children and Youth Leaders** to get their groups/classes involved in some way. Each class/group can make a missions display. Award the best.

13. **Sponsor a Pre-Convention Prayer Meeting**, preferably the weekend prior to convention. Consider: From 7PM to 9PM. By pre-assignment have individuals quietly go to the pulpit on the quarter-hour and present (while people are on their knees praying) a brief, but appropriate Scripture or a need in some foreign field. This nurtures the spirit of prayer.

14. **During Ingathering Sunday, read the INDIVIDUAL Faith Promise amounts** (NOT the names!) from the pulpit as they are gathered a few at a time and brought to you for reading. It will take a bit of time, but the inspirational value is worth that investment! Periodically get subtotals from person working the calculator. Have someone work the "thermometer" at the same time!

15. **Arrange for your Missions Secretary** to read excerpts from a few Missions Letters each month and present graphically, if possible, a report of your Faith Promise giving compared to where you should be at this time. Rejoice if you are even or ahead; pray if you are lagging behind. *Check out "Media and Communication Ideas" by Dale Russo.*

# 3. Policy & Structuring Suggestions

**TERMS:**     How shall we define our Missions focus?
Is it a Missions….**Emphasis?**     Yes, it is. But more!

**Conference?**     A "Conference" is a "thinking" setting. It hears, speaks, and explains ideas, but usually doesn't engage in for making decisions.

**Convention?**     A Convention is an "action" setting. It does all the above, but usually goes beyond a Conference and passes legislation, makes decisions, etc. our preference.

**ASSUMMPTIONS:**

1.   A Faith Promise should represent one's intended giving for _the year_. Leadership informs people of that fact and respects the rule. We ought not say one thing, and then impose another by taking additional offerings when missionaries visit.

2.   With few exceptions, no special offerings should be imposed upon the people who made Faith Promises during the year. Missions emergencies are understandable. But passing the hat when every missionary comes through is an inappropriate imposition on Faith Promise partners, unless congregation is advised of possibility before Convention.

3.   Receiving "love offerings" for visiting missionaries can be problematic. Generally, a charismatic personality, or one serving children, always will get a better response than one doing the less dramatic, like language translation, for example. And it could be the language translator is actually more needy!

4.   Missionaries on the monthly support roster should come by during deputation to report to the people about their ministry on the field- and present needs. Their monthly support is part of their compensation for that ministry, but in addition, he should be sent away with at least a nominal offering from the church's missions budget.

5.   To keep vision alive, it's advisable to appoint someone to regularly read, summarize and report from the monthly missionary newsletters.

6.   A periodic – if not monthly – report informing (and, if possible, with a graph, _showing_) the difference between where missions giving is currently compared to where it should be, is a powerful motivator for prayer and giving.

7.   Faith Promise partners should be encouraged to share with their pastor should they encounter trouble with their Faith Promise. Prayer is still powerful.

8.   If there are a number having difficulty with their Faith Promise, it might be advisable to convene a special prayer service.

9.   It is advisable, but not imperative, that a Missions Department be created by the Pastor and ratified by the Board. It should have its own books, bank account and checks. All checks, however, are to be "invoice- attached" and signatured by a Deacon-Trustee, who is on the Missions Committee. The Committee should be chaired by the Pastor, who shall direct all budgetary and programming events. Both shall be presented to the Board for ratification.

10.  A Missions Committee of not more than seven (7) persons shall be appointed by the Pastor and ratified by the Official Board. It should be representative of the congregation, including youth and women. Their terms, excepting the Secretary-Treasurer, should not be more than two years in succession. The Secretary – Treasurer should be a competent, proven member of the church, He/she should serve a term of three (3) years; then be subject to ratification or replacement. The Secretary-Treasurer shall keep all records accurately and current, including all individual Faith Promise records.

11.  A report of individual giving will be provided to each partner at least twice annually, without asking for money or reflection on the partner, regardless of the amount promised and given.

12.  The recommended length of a convention is _one year_, although there are churches that repeat Faith Promises on a 6 month term. It just seems more efficient to avoid the demands of a "repeat performance" which usually lacks the luster and passion of the first presentation of the year.

# The Faith Promise Concept...

# Marinate in It!

1. Get a Personal word FROM God

2. Give your word TO God

3. ACTIVELY TRUST God to supply it

4. LOOK for it

5. GIVE it !

# Missions Convention Resources

"Any enterprise is built by wise planning,
becomes strong through common sense,
and profits wonderfully by
keeping abreast of the facts."
Proverbs 24:3,4 LB

# 1. A Hypothetical Missions Convention

What follows is only suggestive. It will give you an idea of what your Convention might look like.
Modify to fit your church.

Convention Theme: *"The Time is NOW!"*

Convention Text: "scan the fields, for they are already white for harvesting." John 4:35 Williams Translation

| SUNDAY | WEDNESDAY | FRIDAY EMAIL EMAIL/LETTER | SATURDAY |
|---|---|---|---|
| **Oct. 13**<br>**Sermon: "The Outer Limits"**-Focus on reaching out to others, beyond ourselves, our church.<br>**10 Minute Vignette:** On historic "Haystack Prayer Meeting," the origin of modern missions.<br><br>**PM** Film on World Wide Need/Vision | **16**<br><br>**Focus** on Diversity of Ministries in Missions & Prayer.<br><br>**Film:** themed to Ultimate Destinies of Heaven/Hell<br>**Prayer:** | Pastoral Letters.Email,Facebook<br><br>Initial Letter announcing convention theme, etc (Banquet, Displays, Posters, Prayer,Costume Parade of Nations, etc.) | Brochure on our own or the A/G missions program |
| **Oct. 20**<br>**Sermon: "Bottom Line Religion"**<br>Focus on Ultimate Priorities: Heaven/Hell. "Why should anyone hear Gospel Twice, when so many haven't heard it once?"<br><br>**Vignette:** On David Livingston. Presenter in African dress.<br><br><br><br>**PM** Focus on **AFRICA**. Overview Data from "Mountain Movers" Mag. Specific data/letter/tape from American Missionaries we support. | **23**<br><br>**Focus:**<br>**SKILLS IN MISSIONS**<br>(Sr.Citz., Others on Short Term Missions)<br>**Film:** "Dactar"<br>**PRAYER:** | "We will begin a series this Sunday on the "Components of Missions" This Sun. on Prayer; next Sun. on Personnel & Purse needed to achieve our role in God's Mission. Including brochure on "Faith Promise," a concept that might be new to you, but used of God worldwide. It's simply a way of Partnering with God to raise cash for missions w/o hurting ourselves." | Distribute "Faith Promise" Brochure |
| **Oct. 27**<br>**Sermon: "Components of Missions-Prayer"**<br>**Vignette:** On James Hudson Taylor of **CHINA**, or William Carey of **INDIA**<br><br>**PM** Focus on **ASIA-PACIFIC** | **30**<br>**Focus:**<br>**National Evangelists/ Mass Crusades**<br>**Film:** (Dr. Bob Findlay -"AID")<br>**PRAYER:** | "Why should anyone hear twice, when many haven't heard once? Our Church places priority on unreached, w/o abandoning the "callused ear" at Home, deafened by repeated sound of the Gospel | |
| **NOV.3**<br>Sermon by visiting Missionary "Components of Missions-Personnel"<br><br>Focus on giving oneself for missions. What is in thine hand/heart? How am I personally involved in missions, now?<br>**Song:** "Who will go & work in my fields today?"<br>**Vignette:** Jim Elliot, martyred missionary | **Focus:**<br>**LITERATURE/FILMS**<br>**Film:** "Bullets for the Battle" by World Missionary Press<br><br>Prayer | "The Faith Promise" Provides a crucial ingredient in the "mix" required to fulfill our role for God. Call, Charisma, Character, but also Cash is required.<br>Share Faith Promise victories. | |

| SUNDAY | | | | |
|---|---|---|---|---|
| **Nov. 10**<br>**Sermon: "Components of Missions:**<br>**Purse"**<br><br>**Vignette**: On **David Brainard** reaching the early native Americans. Presenter wears typical Indian clothing: headpiece, etc.<br><br>**All Adult SS Classes:** "The Faith Promise"<br><br>**PM** Focus on **Specialized Ministries** | **13**<br><br>**FOCUS:**<br>**Institutional**<br>**Ministries**<br>(Children/Teen Chall/ Shelters, etc.)<br>**Film:** from A/G Latin America Child Care<br>**PRAYER:** | **Displays/Poster should be completely set up for viewing during Banquet.**<br><br>**BANQUET**<br>Foods of Nations<br><br>**Costume Parade**<br>Graphics:<br>1. Vision -Pastor<br>2. Missions Giv-<br>  ing Chart<br>3. Consecration<br>  of Promise.<br>  Cards. | How does God speak to me? Voice, dream, Word, impression, analysis, 'Ideas for Income.' | **Set up Thermometer**<br>Calculators |
| **NOV. 17**<br>**Sermon: "Creative Faith"**<br>**Kathy: "What shall I give the Master?"**<br><br>**Ingathering of Faith Promises**<br>     (Costumed persons gather FPs.)<br>**Flags/Costume Parade**<br><br>**PM   Ingathering of Balance of FPs** | **20**<br><br>Post to all who registered a Faith Promise, "First Things for Faith Promise Partners" with a cover letter. | | | |

# 2. Planning Grids for Details

# PASTORAL CONCERNS

| | Date | Assigned To: | Follow-Up #1 | #2 |
|---|---|---|---|---|
| **Total Leadership Orientation:** *(Date of Orientation:_____)* | _____ | _____ | _____ | _____ |
| **Ordering:** | | | | |
| 1. Field Posters | _____ | _____ | _____ | _____ |
| 2. Faith Promise Cards | _____ | _____ | _____ | _____ |
| **Costumes** | _____ | _____ | _____ | _____ |
| **Flags** | _____ | _____ | _____ | _____ |
| Dress-up Prep for "Parade" on Saturday Banquet _____ | | _____ | _____ | _____ |
| Dress-up Prep for "Parade" on Saturday Banquet _____ | | _____ | _____ | _____ |
| **Banquet** | _____ | _____ | _____ | _____ |
| Missions Place Matts, etc. | _____ | _____ | _____ | _____ |
| **Visuals:** | | | | |
| 1. Pastor's Vision | _____ | _____ | _____ | _____ |
| 2. Church Faith Promises | _____ | _____ | _____ | _____ |
| **Music** | _____ | _____ | _____ | _____ |

**Pastor's Letters:** Should be mailed each week to reach homes no later than Friday.

**Pastor's Sermons**: Keep integrating theme in messages: "The Time Is NOW"

## 2. *Planning Grids for Details*

Oversight Assigned To:_____

# *DECORATIONS - SANCTUARY, ETC.*

| Item: | Assigned To: | Follow-Up #1 | #2 |
|---|---|---|---|
| **Main Theme Banner** | _____ | _____ | _____ |
| *Set Up* | _____ | _____ | _____ |
| **Posters** | _____ | _____ | _____ |
| Set Up | _____ | _____ | _____ |
| **Flags** | _____ | _____ | _____ |
| Set Up | _____ | _____ | _____ |
| **Thermometer** | _____ | _____ | _____ |
| Set Up | _____ | _____ | _____ |

## 2. *Planning Grids for Details*

Oversight Assigned To:_____

# DISPLAYS / POSTERS/COSTUMES

|  | Assigned To:<br>PERSON | Follow-Up #1<br>DATE | #2<br>DATE |
|---|---|---|---|
| **Displays** | | | |
| Each Sunday School Classes | _____ | _____ | _____ |
| Youth Group | _____ | _____ | _____ |
| Royal Rangers/Boys group | _____ | _____ | _____ |
| Missionettes/Girls group | _____ | _____ | _____ |
| Men's Fellowship | _____ | _____ | _____ |
| WMC | _____ | _____ | _____ |
| Sr. Citizens | _____ | _____ | _____ |
| **Posters** | | | |
| Set Up | _____ | _____ | _____ |
| **Costumes** | | | |
| Locating costumes | _____ | _____ | _____ |

You might want to use costumes in all services, for a Parade of Nations, or a Profile of Nations, using a picture frame as illustrated in next pages; also for Ingathering Sunday

| | | | |
|---|---|---|---|
| Parade of Nations | _____ | _____ | _____ |
| Profile of Nations | _____ | _____ | _____ |
| Narrator | _____ | _____ | _____ |
| Ingathering Sunday | _____ | _____ | _____ |

*An idea of the Profile of Nations can be seen in the pictures that follow.*
*As costumed person stands in the frame, a narrator gives to the people a brief description of the nation he/she represents.*

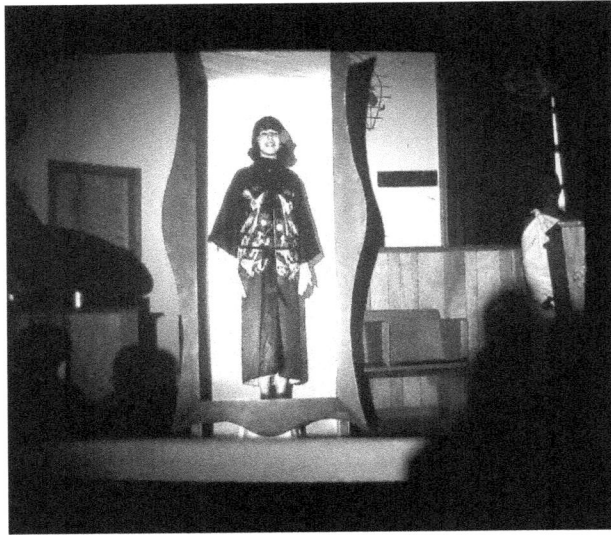

## 2. Planning Grids for Details

# Ministry Assignments:  1

Oversight Assigned To:_____

# SUNDAY AM MISSIONARY SPEAKERS

| DATE | MISSIONARY'S NAME | FIRST CALL | FOLLOW-UP |
|------|-------------------|------------|-----------|
| _____ | _____ | _____ | _____ |
| _____ | _____ | _____ | _____ |
| _____ | _____ | _____ | _____ |
| _____ | _____ | _____ | _____ |
| _____ | _____ | _____ | _____ |
| _____ | _____ | _____ | _____ |
| _____ | _____ | _____ | _____ |

## 2. Planning Grids for Details

# Ministry Assignments:2

Oversight Assigned To:_____

# MISSIONARY STATESMEN VIGNETTES

|  | Date | Assigned To: | Follow-Up #1 | #2 |
|---|---|---|---|---|
| "Haystack Prayer Meeting: | _____ | _____ | _____ | _____ |
| David Livingston: | _____ | _____ | _____ | _____ |
| James Hudson Taylor | _____ | _____ | _____ | _____ |
| William Carey | _____ | _____ | _____ | _____ |
| Jim Elliot | _____ | _____ | _____ | _____ |
| David Brainard | _____ | _____ | _____ | _____ |

Presenter of above People should appear dressed as person represented.
See person assigned to Costumes/Flags for assistance.

## 2. Planning Grids for Details

# Ministry Assignments: 3.

Oversight Assigned To:_____

# SUNDAY EVENING: FIELD OVERVIEWS

| | Date | Assigned To: | Follow-Up #1 | #2 |
|---|---|---|---|---|
| Oct.13: World Overview | _____ | _____ | _____ | _____ |
| 20: Africa | _____ | _____ | _____ | _____ |
| 27: Asia-Pacific | _____ | _____ | _____ | _____ |
| Nov. 3: Latin America | _____ | _____ | _____ | _____ |
| 10: Specialized Ministries | _____ | _____ | _____ | _____ |

Presenter should get data about missionaries your church supports in the Field he represents, and share that data with the people.

A "Three Minute" taped Greeting from the missionary is helpful; requested in advance, either by Pastor or by Presenter.

## 2. *Planning Grids for Details*

# *Ministry Assignments: 4*

Oversight Assigned To:_____

# SCHEDULING WEDNESDAY NIGHT FILMS/VIDEOS

| For Use : (date) | From: | Assigned To: | Follow-Up #1 | #2 |
|---|---|---|---|---|
| _____ : **"Ultimate Decision"** Gospel Films<br>*Projector Operator* | | _____<br>_____ | _____<br>_____ | ____<br>____ |
| _____ : **"Dactar"** Gospel Films<br>Projector Operator | | _____<br>_____ | _____<br>_____ | ____<br>____ |
| _____ : **"National Evangelists"** "AID" Bob Findley<br>Projector Operator | | _____<br>_____ | _____<br>_____ | ____<br>____ |
| _____ : **"Bullets for the Battle:** Missionary Press<br>Projector Operator | | _____<br>_____ | _____<br>_____ | ____<br>____ |
| _____ : **Children in Need** *LA Child Care*<br>Projector Operator | | _____<br>_____ | _____<br>_____ | ____<br>____ |

For the best ministry, all necessary media equipment should be set up at least half hour before service is to start, and that a test run has been made to assure "flawless" presentation.

**NOTE: Film titles are only suggestive.** Online search will offer great variety; also denominational missions departments, etc.

# 3. Bibliography
## on The Faith Promise

**Note:** The fact that there have been no recent publications on the Faith Promise subject suggests there has been little sober reflection on this subject.
Although some of the publications listed above are from the 60s & 70s their content is still helpful.

Cooper, Clay, "Your Home Church and Its Foreign Mission," Moody Press, Chicago, Ill.
© 1963

Reeves, Robert E., "Faith Promise: a missions success story," Standard Publishing, Cincinnati, OH, No © date   Publication No. 2862

Lewis, Ph.D., Norman, "Faith Promise," Western Conservative Baptist Seminary, Portland Oregon 97215 © 1973

Lewis, Ph.D., Norman, "Faith Promise for World Missions – a Handbook," Back to the Bible Broadcast, Box 82808, Lincoln, Nebraska  68501   © 1974

Lewis, Ph.D., Norman, "Triumphant Missionary Ministry in the Local Church," Back to the Bible Publishers, Box 233, Lincoln 1, Nebraska      ©1961

Smith, Paul B., "The Senders" World Missions Conferences and Faith promise Offerings, G.R. Welch Company, Limited, Toronto, Canada  © 1979  ISBN:0-919532-53-5

Jensen, Donald A., "Your Church Can Excel in Global Giving; the Faith Promise Way to a Dynamic Outreach"

Brown, James, "Faith Promise and Beyond"

# 4. Letters & Stories
## of Faith Promise Success

### "Just give me an idea"

"After I made my Faith Promise, I went home thinking: 'Now Lord, how am I going to get this money?' I knew I shouldn't ask my husband, Bob. And I'm not talented so I could sit down and make something to sell. So I said: 'Lord, you just give me an idea.'

"One day, Bob said, 'You know, we've got so much 'junk' in this house. Why don't you have a garage sale?' And it dawned on me! This is what the Lord wanted me to do for my Faith Promise.

"I worked for three days getting things ready, with the help of my Uncle who was skeptical about what I was doing since he didn't believe like we do.

"Even before I opened my garage door to officially open the sale, people came to me and I made my first $100.00! Without even trying, it came in. It was so easy. I teased my Uncle: 'Now, we don't even have to open the garage door. It will all be sold before I put my posters out!' But we did. And as it turned out, I made over $400.00.

"Believe me. That really boosted my faith. In fact, making a Faith Promise actually strengthened my faith so I was able to handle a crises that later came into our family."
-D.B. Youngstown, OH

### "It was such a sweet surprise!"

"Enclosed is a check toward my Faith Promise.

"I wish to explain briefly that this money came to me completely unexpectedly. I had a terminal patient who knowingly began to prepare to die. She was a retired nurse, who knew cancer was too widespread for any possible help. I began to deal with her spiritually and prayerfully that God would save her. She considered all things, began to seek the Lord and confessed her love for Jesus. and confessed she felt His presence in her room. It was a joy to see her love. She was calm, patient, and loving toward me.

"After she died, her husband wrote me a sweet not of thanks 'for what I had done with his wife' —and enclosed a $50.00 bill. I immediately thanked God and remembered my Faith Promise! It was such a sweet surprise to me! The Lord is wonderful."
-M.C Arlington, Mass.

## "Don't ever say, it can't be done!"

"This past year has proven to me when you promise in faith and trust in the Lord, He always provides. I promised $500.00 and didn't have any money and my working condition was very poor. I only worked 6 months out of 12. When I became discouraged and didn't know where to turn the mail would come and there would be $100.00 or another time someone would hand me money.

"I could of used this money for my household expenses but gave it toward my Faith Promise and each time I gave toward my Faith Promise, the Lord would provide with another gift through the mail or from another unexpected source. So, with the faithfulness of the Lord I paid off my Faith Promise without taking any from my own budget. So, don't be afraid to trust in the Lord because when you are faithful to Him, He never lets you down."
-R.C. Greenville, PA.

## "...because it was His figure!"

"About a year ago, as I was sitting in the Sunday morning worship service during our Missions Convention, the Lord began dealing with me to make a Faith Promise. Several figures popped into my mind, but one stood out because it was HIS figure.

"I thought, 'well, why not go ahead and try it.' Months went by and the money wasn't around and I began to worry, argue and complain with myself on why I promised such a figure. How stupid I was! I finally decided, (which I should have done all along) to pray and seek God for the answer because His Word says He is a very present help in trouble – and I felt I was in trouble!

"It then came to me as I was preparing my Income Tax that my return was $100.00 greater than it had been in the 10 years I worked. I thought, 'O Lord! Here it is! The answer! So simple!' When I received my check, I turned it over for my Faith Promise and still had some left for my own use.

"I praise God for teaching me how to wait upon Him for the answer, a lesson that I needed to learn."
-Greenville, PA

## "I doubled my Faith Promise"

"Since the time I made a Faith promise God has blessed me financially. My salary was raised by almost (40%) forty percent. Praise God! Therefore I have doubled my Faith Promise. Truly, it is impossible to out-give God!!
-VS Niles, OH

## "...and then some!"

"I made a Faith Promise at convention not knowing for sure that I had a job and knowing that if I did have a job, it would be at my old salary (pre-military service). The day after I made my Faith Promise I called the hospital and found that I did have a job, and that I was going to start at a salary about $1300.00 more than had been expected. Praise the Lord! He provided the money for my Faith Promise and then some! How gloriously God provides when we reach out in faith. Thanks for presenting the opportunity."
-F.P. Aliquippa, PA

## "...not having any problems"

"I'm not having any problems meeting my missionary Faith Promise. God has sent so many piano and organ students my way that I can't take them all and I have a waiting list."
-A.G. Lincoln Park, Mich.


## "I could not touch this. This is God's money."

Randy Hurst tells an inspiring about a young graduate from a Bible School in Mbeya, Tanzania, started by Hurst's father. Enose made a Faith Promise before he went to Songwe to plant a church. A few weeks later, Hurst's father decided to visit the young preacher, now living some 40 miles distant. He found him stomping mud preparing bricks for the church he planned to build. After greeting the elder Hurst, Enose ran into his house and returned with 30 shillings, about a week's wages. It was for the Faith Promise he had made. As Hurst was about to leave he remembered he had purchased some food for Enose. When he saw it, Enose was ecstatic! "Surely, God sent you today! I have not had food for three days." Hurst 's response was understandable. "But Enose, if you had money, why didn't you bury food?" Enose answered, "I could not touch this. This is God's money."
-Randy Hurst in brochure: "What is a Faith Promise?"

# 5
# *Sources for Videos & Films*
# Websites

CHURCH OF THE NAZARENE                                http://home.snu.edu/~hculbert/videos.htm

ASSEMBLIES OF GOD WORLD MISSIONS DEPT.:    www.ag.org

GATEWAY FILMS VISION VIDEO:                       https://www.visionvideo.com
 CHRISTIAN REFORMED WORLD MISSIONS:         www.crcna.org/pages/crwm.cfm

BMS WORLD MISSIONS:                         http://www.bmsworldmissions.org/resources/giving

# 6. Statistics:
# The Unfinished Challenge

**AS OF APRIL 2012:**

▶ There were approximately 7 billions people on Earth

▶ About 750 million (or about 11%) of the 7 billion claim Jesus as personal Lord and Savior

▶ About 2.6 billion people (or 38%) of the 7 billion) have heard the Gospel, but have not accepted Jesus

▶ Just over 50% (or 3.5 billion people) have not heard the Gospel and most of them do not have opportunity to hear the Gospel

**ANOTHER WAY TO LOOK AT THE CHALLENGE OF WORLD EVANGELISM:**

▶ Of the 11, 646 distinct people groups on the planet, 6,734 people groups (roughly 60%) contain between zero and two percent evangelical Christians. Many of these 6,734 people groups have no churches, no Bible, no Christian literature, and no mission agencies who are seeking to share the Gospel with them.

**RESOURCES FOR ADDITIONAL STATISTICAL DATA:**

www.**globalchristianity**.org – *Gordon Conwell*

*www.message**missions**.com/**missionstatistics**/*

www.joshuaproject.net/great-com**mission-statistics**.

*www.about**missions**.org/**statistics**.html*

www.thetravelingteam.org/**stats**

# 7. Media and Communication Ideas

By
Dale Russo, Executive Director of Missions,
*International Fellowship of Christian Assemblies*

1.

Do a news flash type skit giving info while showing pictures from the mission field that deals with your report on the screen that you have. Pick one bit of information for each missionary from the up-date reports that shows progress, vision, or answer to prayer, etc... Someone could read a short script explaining the appropriate pictures. Or do a parity on the View using missionary reports; a Jay Leno/Dave Letterman type interview using the missionary reports as the substance, Bill O'Reily etc.

The staff could have a small set built like Fox news and either broadcast live (roll the set onto the stage or dedicate a spot on the stage for it) or tape a segment during the week and play it sometime during the service via video projector. This could be monthly or bi-weekly up-date. Have the entire up-date report available in the foyer for those who would want to know more. This could involve a variety of people within the church.

If you choose to do a taping, several backdrops could be made so that each time a different venue could be used. ***Be creative and very catchy.***

2.

Do a running banner of information on the top or bottom of the screen using the video projector during the announcements and offering without pictures or with the corresponding pictures like Fox News does during their news shows. Again, edit down the info to one thing per missionary. This could be weekly, bi-weekly, or monthly. Have available the full composite report in the foyer for those who would want to know more.

3.

Send out a mass email to all those parishioners whose addresses you have in your data base. This could be done with simple editing of information into bullets with the appropriate picture instead of body text to provide just a summary. This could be done as up-dates are received.

If you do the video idea, you could send it as a mass email attachment that your people could forward to their friends or show church people who do not have email what the church is up to.

4.

Dedicate a place in the foyer for missions that is high traffic area and set up a screen showing number 1 or 2 and post the info in 1/2 page readable form or bullets that they can take with them to read in more full details. Make the full composite report available for those who want to know more.

5.
Dedicate one Sunday a month as Missions Sunday when such information is stressed in a variety of ways on a variety of levels and in a variety of ministries.

6.
The up-date reports could be edited into bullet form to be passed out at home groups and etc.

7.
The video of #2 could be made on a DVD RW and distributed to the home groups, other groups and all your ministries throughout the church.

8.
The up-date reports could be edited into bullet form and copied as an insert to the bulletin. Or, one significant story from each missionary could be printed in full from the up-date report. The bulletin insert then could have 2, 3 depending upon how much each story needed and how many stories one side of the insert will hold. I would have a special design made for the other side of the bulletin insert that reflects World Missions: Accelerating the Gospel. It should be eye catching. Then the people will associate that insert with missions and know something of significance is printed on the other side.

"And Jesus came and spake
unto them, saying,
All power is given unto me
in heaven and in earth."

"Go ye therefore,
and teach all nations,

baptizing them
in the name of the Father,
and of the Son,
and of the Holy Ghost:

Teaching them to observe

all things whatsoever I have commanded you:
and, lo,
I am with you always,

Even unto the end of the world.
Amen.

Matthew 28:18 - 20

# The Faith Promise Concept...

# Teach It!

1.  Get a Personal word FROM God

2.  Give your word TO God

3.  ACTIVELY TRUST God to supply it

4.  LOOK for it

5.  GIVE it !

# Reprintables

# 1. Text of The Narration

One of the most amazing gifts God has given Christians is the ability to trust Him to supply money for missions, frequently supernaturally.  In fact, you can  give to missions  money you don't have from sources you don't  even know about.

Allow me to repeat that one more time: You can give to missions money you don't have from sources you don't even know about.  Thousands are doing just that.

♦-Like the teenager who gave $60.00 even though she didn't even have a  babysitting job.

♦-Or the college student who didn't have money for tuition but gave $100.00.

♦-And the young unemployed Mother of four who gave $1000.00.

♦-Or the church with less than 15 families and in a $250,000.00 building   program, yet gave thousands for missions.

How did they do it?

They surely didn't do it by economic power because it simply wasn't there!  They did it by the power of a gift God gave them.  And the good news is that this same powerful gift is _already inside you_.  The Bible tells us that "to every person is given a measure of faith."  God put it there!  Like a magnificent diamond of enormous value and wonderful potential. Within it is miraculous power, and with it - under the Lord's leadership -- you can give to missions monies you don't have from sources you don't even know about.

God wants you to unlock that gift and put it to work for His Kingdom.  If it lies dormant and remains hidden inside you, no one ever can be blest by its beauty and value.  Permit me to say that when you release your gift of faith, you will know it, and so will everyone else!  Real faith gives proof and shows substance. It's more than pretty words and warm, fuzzy feelings. It sparkles like a diamond when you use it and is incredibly valuable when you cash-it-in. It will be unmistakable!

The exciting thing about your faith is that you actually can convert it into Money for Missions even though it often seems impossible & even irrational because there is no visible source to get that money.      But you do have faith! And Jesus said, "According to your faith be it unto you." So, it's clear.  If you will partner with God in missions, that magnificent diamond in your heart – your faith - will make a big difference in our world.

*The Key is for you to get a word from the Lord*.  Let Him whisper in your heart how much money He wants you to trust Him to provide for missions. What He tells you is *God's Promise to you*. And He will supply it, even if it takes a miracle!

Once you get that word from the Lord, you need to register it on a Faith Promise card.  That's *your promise to God*.  That's what we call a Faith Promise.

It's _not_ a pledge that someone will try to collect from you. It's just your promise that you will trust the Lord to provide what He said He would, and that you will give it to missions as He provides.

It's giving according to your faith, _not_ according to money you have in your pocket, your budget or bank account. For that all you have to do is just reach into your pocket and give it!  Your Faith Promise is a record of what you are trusting God to supply for missions because of the word He gave you.

How much you should register on your Faith Promise is strictly between you and God alone. Whether you are a child, a teenager, young adult, unemployed, retired senior citizen or challenged, you can give to Missions because God will tell you personally what to give. It's your *personal* adventure with God. Only He can tell you what to believe for, and you alone must determine how much it should be, in your own way.

Some folks claim God tells them how much to give in an audible voice. Some have dreams. Most get a strong impression or deep inner conviction about what they should give.  Still others suddenly "discover" a number in their mind; and some just figure it out by considering possibilities while trusting God to lead them.  But everyone gets their own personal word from the Lord. Nobody can do that for you.

Sometimes in the process, some folks realize they really need to scale down their wish- list of toys and trinkets, adjust their priorities and perhaps refocus their goals as well as rework their budget to reflect a heart sensitive to the pain and privation millions in the world suffer.  It might not be easy, but remembering Calvary can help.

It's not unusual in this adventure with God for Him to drop into our minds creative ways to get the money we need for missions.

He has given "Ideas for Income" that literally have generated thousands of dollars for Missions. Mrs. B in Youngstown, OH got an idea about what her husband called the "junk" in her attic and basement, and through a garage sale converted it into several hundred dollars cash for missions. Another lady, who raised African Violets as a hobby, got the bright idea of selling them.  For many years those pretty little flowers supported third world pastors & evangelists!  The idea God gave a man in Texas was to raise a steer for missions. From one, he went to two; then three; then more. And eventually, Steer, Inc., emerged as a powerful supplier of monies for missions.  It was similar to the man who designed "Praying Hands" jewelry and ended up with a gift store in Hubbard, OH. The ideas for income God inspires are just amazing!

Usually, people who register Faith Promises are encouraged to tell their Pastor if they are having trouble with them. A man in one church, who was led to register a Faith Promise based on earnings from his bee hives, told his Pastor rather bluntly one day he was pouring more sugar into his hives to keep the bees alive than what they were worth.  His Pastor encouraged him and asked him to pray with him about this challenge to his faith.  When he saw him again a few weeks later, the man said, "I don't know what you did Pastor, but it sure worked. Now I'm having a hard time keeping up with them adding layers to the hives!" That season when most bee keepers in Mercer County, PA struggled with their bees, Paul had a "bumper crop!" His Faith Promise was challenged. But God came through as He always does!

It's not unusual for folks to wonder if giving to missions will hurt local church giving.  The opposite is true.  Actually, local church giving usually increases.

It happened in Niagara Falls, NY when a church gathered Faith Promises for several thousand dollars far beyond their usual giving and were pleasantly surprised when the folks generously gave _additional monies_ to build a new parsonage. Giving to missions didn't hurt them!

44

It also happened in Youngstown, OH. Right in the middle of a two-hundred thousand dollar building program, the church dared to believe God and they witnessed record-breaking giving for Missions without hurting their budget. Some said it couldn't be done, but they did it because they released their faith in the word the Lord gave them.

And It happened in Rochester, N.Y, too, in a Three Year old church. Although they were in a quarter of a million dollar building program, their bold faith registered missions Faith Promises for thousands of dollars. God gave them the word, supplied the money and they gave!

Now, it doesn't seem presumptuous to suggest you are watching this presentation because you have a heart for God, and that you would like to partner with Him in Missions. The fact is: you've already got what it takes. So, let me tell you how you can translate that diamond of faith into money you don't have from sources you don't even know about:

1. Get a word from God. Find a private place where He can bring His word to you without distraction. Consider possible ways He might supply money for missions through you. Be open to any "Idea for Income" He might drop into your heart. Settle on an amount of money you believe He wants you to trust Him to supply through you. Whether its one dollar, a thousand or more - that will be the amount of your Faith Promise for the year.

2. Record your Faith Promise. This gives proof of your faith that God will supply the money, and that you will give it as it comes in. What you register will be added with all the Faith Promises to set the church's goal for the year. The total also shows the church's real faith-level for missions.

3. Actively trust God for it. You might experience a trial of your faith. But don't despair. Keep praying and trusting, even if the situation seems irrational, impossible and there is no visible source of supply. Remember the bee keeper!

4. Be on the "Look-out" for it! "Extra" monies can come in the most unexpected ways. Even usual holidays & celebrations can be times for supplying your Faith Promise goal. When new "Ideas for Income" come along, work them diligently!

5. Read the labels right! As the money comes in give it. Julie registered a Faith Promise for one thousand dollars. It was humanly impossible for this young mother to come up with that

kind of money. But she believed God wanted her to trust Him for it- and she did. Now, nearly a year has past. Not a cent came in.

Then three weeks before the missions convention year ended in her church, her grandfather unexpectedly died. And just as unexpectedly, he left her two gold coins. The appraiser said they were valued at exactly one thousand dollars!

Now with one thousand dollars in hand and facing all the things their children needed for the new school year as well as some necessary house repairs, she and her husband struggled abou giving it for missions. The temptation was real and understandable, but so was their commitment.

They knew the money was marked for missions. It was money they didn't have. It was supplied by God from a source they didn't even know about. And they did give it for missions.

----------------------

As believers partner with God in World Missions, faith victories like this are revolutionizing Missions giving. Their Faith Promises are dramatically increasing money for missions and inspiring laborers to enter the harvest field. More importantly, they are healing the hurting and saving the lost.

My Friend, please consider being a part of this exciting team.
Give the Lord an opportunity to make a promise to you.
Then make your promise to God by registering a Faith Promise.

Thanks for being on the team.

You are appreciated.

# 2. Brochures

The Faith Promise: Q & A

The Faith Promise Didn't Work for US

What to do When Your Faith Promise is in Trouble

First Things for Faith Promise Partners

# Note:

## Download all Brochures from the DVD

# 1. WHAT IS A FAITH PROMISE?

▲ It is a written record of a certain sum of money one believes the Lord will help him give to missions in the next year because the Lord impressed that amount on his mind & he knows God keeps His Word, even if he has to do a miracle.

▲ It is a missions tool with which you Cash-in your faith for money and become a partner with God in World Evangelism.

-It doesn't touch your pocketbook, bank account, or savings – the cash you have. (He may ask you to modify your standard of living if its too high!) But the Faith Promise involves only money you believe God to provide for missions.

▲ It is a Missions Tool based on Bible-kind of faith.

-Bible Faith is not needed where money is in your pocket, your savings account, or when your budget can afford it. Bible-kind of faith is for when you face:
   ... the Impossible,
   ... the Unreasonable, and
   ... the Unknown.

▲ It is PROOF of how much you REALLY believe that God is your supply and partner in winning the lost.

-You have Bible-kind of faith. How far you will stretch it is the challenge. "According to your faith be it unto you."

▲ It is a promise To God, based on His promise TO YOU...that you will give to missions the money He provides.

▲

# 2. HOW DO YOU WORK IT?

▲ Get a Money-Figure from the Lord. Wait quietly on Him and let Him impress on your mind how much money He wants you to trust Him to provide to you for missions in the next year.

-He might give you an Idea for Income. Put it to work! Not all miracle money drops out of the sky. Remember the widow with the cruse of oil? She worked her Idea for Income.

▲ Write that Money-Figure on your Faith Promise Card...because you believe God will supply it somehow, even though it now looks:
   ...Impossible
   ...Unreasonable, and the Means is
   ...Unknown.

▲ Pray about it daily. Expect miracles!

▲ Be alert to unexpected monies that come in or unexpected opportunities to earn it.

▲ Give the money as the Lord provides it. (Beware of embezzling the Lord's money!)

# 3. WHO SHOULD MAKE ONE?

▲ Every Christian whose faith is not dead; especially leaders of groups. Mothers, Dads, collegians, teenagers, children. Certainly Pastors, Evangelists, Sunday School Teachers, Church Officers. Many businessmen make one for their business.

-It' surprising how many church leaders have no personal method for giving systematically to missions!

-It's "according to your faith"

# 4. WILL I BE BADGERED TO GIVE OTHER MISSIONS OFFERINGS?

▲ No. This is it. In a Missions Convention your Faith Promise Card is totaled with others to see what your church goal is for the year. That's your faith-level starring right at you! The annual budget is based on this total. Visiting missionaries and regular missions programs are covered by this income. *Except for emergency or special divine guidance*, no other offerings are taken for missions. You just give your Faith Promise as the money comes in.

# 5. IS THERE ANY PROOF THAT IT WORKS?

Stacks of it. Here are a few examples:

COLLEGIAN: "When I made my faith promise I had no idea where the money would come from...God gave me a 'buyer' for a course I couldn't complete for the amount of my Faith Promise....it was unusual...It was money I would have otherwise lost."

SOCIAL WORKER: "Since I made my faith promise, my salary was raised by almost 40%, Praise God! Therefore I have doubled my faith promise."

HOUSE WIFE: "My Catholic neighbor came over and asked if I would launder the altar linens for her church. I paid off my Fait Promise with the money."

"Why should anyone hear the Gospel twice, when so many have not heard it once?"

*....the Word*

"*Remember this:* Whoever sows sparingly, will also reap sparingly and whoever sows generously will also reap generously. Each man should give what he has decided in his heart to give, not reluctantly or under compulsion, for God loves a cheerful giver. And God is able to make all grace abound to you, so that in all things at all times, having all that you need, you will abound in every good work....

This service that you perform is not only supplying the needs of God's people but is also overflowing in many expressions of thanks to God...And in their prayers for you their hearts will go out to you, because of the surpassing grace God has given you. Thanks be to God for his indescribable gift."

**2 Corinthians 9:6-15**

---

## 6. CAN IT HURT OUR LOCAL CHURCH ?

▶ No! Money you never had can't be taken away. In fact, the Faith Promise will help. Surveys show churches that do not use the Faith Promise actually deny themselves a unique source of extra income. Tithes of good church members make sure there is "meat in mine house," says the Lord of Hosts. The Faith Promise is money He provides in addition to the usual tithes. It's "outside" money.

-A small Missouri church increased its current budget income from $4600.00 to $6032.00 in one year after making Faith Promises for Missions.
-**An Illinois church increased current budget giving by $5000.00 over a four year period.**
-An Ohio church experienced increased current income even though they held their first missions convention during a $250,000.00 construction project.

## 7. HOW DOES MY TITHE FIT IN ?

▶ You pay your tithe "off-the-top" of your usual source of income. It's your way of honoring God's Fatherly care for your daily needs. With your Faith Promise, you go beyond God's Paternalism & join with Him as a Partner in world evangelism as He provides special monies.

## 8. WHAT HAPPENS IF I CAN'T PAY IT OFF ?

▶ Nothing! That's what makes it different from a Pledge. Pledges can e collected if necessary, even by legal means. It makes you accountable to men. With a Faith Promise you explain your situation only to God. After all, He put the amount of money on your heart to begin with! Faith Promise partners will encourage & pray with you. But your business is with God alone.

---

# FAITH PROMISE

## What Questions Do You Ask Before Making A

1. What is it?
2. How do you work it?
3. Who should make one?
4. Will I be badgered to give other missions offerings this year?
5. Is there any proof that it works?
6. Won't it hurt our local church finances?
7. How does my tithe fit in?
8. What happens if I can't pay it off?

**An introduction to the Revolutionary Concept of giving that has provided millions of dollars for world evangelism while strengthening the local church.**

A mountain of evidence illustrates the dramatic effectiveness of the Faith Promise concept in providing money for missions. But occasionally, people are encountered whose experience suggests the Faith Promise didn't work. At least, they allege it didn't work for them.

Exactly why the Faith Promise didn't work for them is a highly personal thing; and the pursuit of specific causes probes the deepest sources of motivation, which to the best of us, becomes a most elusive venture because of the discomforting nature of the search. Nevertheless, a few more obvious causes can be suggested for the ostensible failure of the Faith Promise

## A WORD FROM THE LORD

A major consideration is whether one, in fact, had an *accurate* word of guidance from the Lord. This is, of course, basic to the Faith Promise. It calls for trusting the Lord to provide what *the Lord* indicated He would supply. "If ye abide in me and *my word* abide in you...it shall be given unto thee." Unfortunately, we are not as skilled at discerning His will as we would like to be. All of us are yet "going to school" – in the learning process. From that standpoint, the Faith Promise is *experimental* rather than absolute. Consequently, at times, we are carried away by the good, but misguided sentiments of our humanity, prompted by overly dramatized world need or a rather careless emphasis upon our prerogatives as God's people.

World need is no surprise to God; neither will He be coerced by wishful thinking, illusionary faith or grandioso imagination to do what He has not predetermined to do. Partnership with God in world evangelism, be it ever so noble, is not license for dictating to God. It's imperative that one gets *His* word of guidance if one's Faith Promise is to be fulfilled.

## IDEAS FOR INCOME

The matter of putting to work Ideas for Income which God gives is also related to a successful Faith Promise. Experience shows it doesn't always please the Father to send ravens with divine supply to drop manna from Heaven. More often than not, He gives birth to an idea which, if acted upon can generate income for one's Faith Promise. And *this* idea needn't necessarily originate with the person himself. The Lord has been known to speak a creative suggestion through another. Like the husband, who upon returning from work one late afternoon, casually suggested to his wife that a garage sale might "get rid of" much of the good but unneeded "stuff" cluttering their home. The woman immediately recognized God as the source of the idea. But it didn't "pay off" without good hard work, dragging items from the attic, scrubbing them up, and selling them off!

## READ THE LABELS RIGHT

One of the more subtle reasons Faith Promises occasionally don't work lies in our tendency to misread the labels on money our Lord does provide through the year. We are too prone to assume God's way is always the sensational way. So that if money comes to us in ordinary ways like our birthdays, or Christmas, or we are awarded an increase in wages – or experience some increase in "one-of-a-million" ordinary ways – somehow we conclude those monies don't apply to our Faith Promises!

## SUBTLE DETOURS

In a sense, related to this practice is the strong temptation to misappropriate Faith promise funds for personal and family use. This is especially true when the money coming to us is a large sum. There are always personal and family needs and at times, other non-personal uses – to which Faith Promise money can be applied. Unless great care is taken in this regard, one can easily rationalize "detouring" God's supply and fall prey to embezzling funds that the Lord of Harvest supplied for the support of missions.

Either one or a combination of these factors can contribute to unfulfilled Faith Promises. The conscientious Christian will carefully evaluate his own performance in the light of these factors and carefully avoid "blaming" God for failing to meet an obligation to which earlier the Christian said God had committed Himself. In this way he can prevent a debilitating cloud of unbelief from forming over a tool the Lord of Harvest has effectively employed to raise literally millions of dollars for world missions. We must remember: God is true to His Word!

The Faith Promise is part of one's development as a disciple of Christ. He ought not be discouraged from future use of this powerful missionary tool because of an initial or occasional failure. These are growing pains. Disciples are learners. And this expertise also shall be learned! It seems to me this is what the writer to the Hebrews had in mind when he observed disciples who "are of full age," that is, mature or accomplished in working with God. They achieved that level of personal development because they "exercised their senses" and "by reason of (such) use" developed skills for discerning the will of God accurately. (Hebrews 5:14) The familiar cliché expresses well an appropriate word of encouragement: "Practice makes perfect!" It applies to the the Faith Promise concept, too. ♥

World need is no surprise to God; neither will He be coerced by wishful thinking, illusionary faith or grandioso imagination to do what He has not predetermined to do

©Life Enrichment Ministries, Inc.
EMAIL: GuyBon@zoominternet.net

# The Faith Promise Didn't Work For Us

## Insights to Failure

By
**Guy BonGiovanni, D. Min.**

# What to do when your Faith Promise is in trouble

- tell it to the Lord
- keep your ear to the ground

lesser interests. Recorders or cell phones are fine. So is a new bicycle or automobile. And even a new dining room set is better than the one you've had for several years but can yet serve you well, and that with honor. Using God's supply on these things, however, is a misappropriation of funds when the Faith Promise is incomplete—that is, if your priorities are right. Lamenting a lack of money to complete the Faith Promise....and even subtly blaming God for it....under such circumstances can lead to trouble in your life of faith. Keep your priorities right.

Seriously now, do you think God would lead you to make an annual Faith Promise of $125.00 and then let you down? Not for the work closest His heart! Your partnership with God is a prized relationship. It means the difference of hundreds of people saved or lost to Him Who is "NOT willing that ANY should perish." If He has to do a miracle to supply it, He will. Tell it to Him again in prayer. Through your prayer and faith you can move circumstances to bless the world with salvation in Christ.

Keep your ear to the ground! Be alert to opportunities....every opportunity. Grab them up! Make the miracle happen. It's indisputably true: He is "able to do exceeding abundantly above all that we ask or think, according to the power that worketh in us."

*"ATTEMPT* GREAT THINGS FOR GOD. *EXPECT* GREAT THING *FROM GOD"*
- William Carey

©Life Enrichment Ministries, Inc.
EMAIL: GuyBon@zoominternet.net

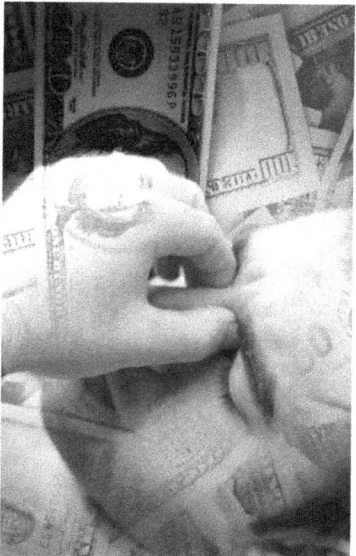

Some of the most exciting experiences of life are to be had as a Partner with God in World Evangelism through the use of a Faith Promise. It's thrilling to watch God supply money for missions and arrange circumstances so money can be earned. But you need to keep your ear to the ground!

Novel writers of the Old West made famous the legendary Indian practice of putting their ear to the ground. Through her vibrations, Mother Earth supposedly transferred both the number and distance of approaching friend or foe. Perhaps this is more fiction than fact. Nevertheless, it graphically portrays the keen and constant powers of perception God's partners need if their Faith Promises are not to fail. They must be alert.

In any venture of faith, a keen sense of spiritual discernment is needed....and the Faith Promise venture is no exception. It must equally register Heaven-sent impulses of guidance and Providentially arranged "worldly" opportunities. The source of supply must be seen not only in God-directed ravens dropping bread in the Prophet's lap, but in the privileges for "work by the sweat of thy brow" as well. Such understanding is required for a successful and satisfying partnership in World Evangelism using the Faith Promise.

**TELL IT TO THE LORD**

The Faith Promise is an agreement between God's co-worker and Himself. Except for recording the Faith Promise annually, no accounting of it is given to any man. It is not a pledge. This is strictly a private affair with God.

God impressed you with a definite amount of money you could believe Him to supply for World Evangelism, weekly, monthly, or annually. You agreed to pray, believe and work for this amount as He either miraculously sent it in or through circumstances gave opportunity to earn it. The Promise was recorded by faith that expected to fully satisfy the annual amount. There was no doubt then. Now, however, you wonder if you can keep it up....money is not available. "What can I do?" you ask.

**TELL IT TO THE LORD!** After all, you were convinced He led you to trust Him for it. And World Evangelism is in fact the work of God's greatest interest in our world. So why not tell it to the Lord in prayer. "ASK and it shall be given unto you. SEEK and ye shall find. KNOCK and it shall be opened unto you." That's exactly what the Lord of Harvest urged us to do. It might be: 'ye have not because ye ask not.'

**BE ALERT**

But more than that...REMEMBER the Indian legend. Keep your ear to the ground! Be creative. Be alert to every opportunity.

A little steer was pastured on the plains near Park River, North Dakota. A year later, the profit it brought above its cost on the auction block was used for missions. The idea developed. STEER, a nationwide organization "STEERING Money to Missions" was born because E. V. Folden, a man with missions in his heart, kept his ear to the ground.

In Slatington, Pa., Mrs. Harry Steckel came up with her partnership by raising violets. Her "Violet Fund" began with a "baby" taken from a relative's African Violet plant. "For the past 14 years, I've sold more than 3,000 plants and have had as many as 500 plants at one time," Said Mrs. Steckel. The only plant this lady with a "green thumb" ever bought had but four leaves. "But any way, it grew," she said with satisfaction. Grow it did! Among other things it grew big enough to support Chinese war orphans for more than 7 years at $120.00 a year. A bit different from raising steer, but it helps get the job of evangelism done!

These champions of faith told God, to be sure. But they also kept their ears to the ground. With Keen discernment they knew their opportunity — and God's — and they grasped it for the sake of the unsaved.

**LITTLE IS MUCH**

Too frequently folks wait for the "big one" and in the process lose it all. Through little insignificant used postage stamps, $2,100.00 was invested in one year for a Gospel Literature Program by the Libreria La Aurora, a Latin American organization.

Little things....and used things can be redeemed for missionary value when they lose their practical and sentimental value to you personally. Like the Indian Head coin collection which took hours of tedious work to compile....like the diamond- studded wedding ring left as an heirloom by a departed wife and mother....or like the wallet with several stray bills found by a wife after her husband was called Home to God.

Look around you at the things you possess in the attic, in the basement... some closet. Are there unused commodities? Redeem them for cash to complete your Faith Promise. Not just large gifts....little things like the gold in old jewelry....antiques....musical instruments....good equipment of various sorts. Alertness here, too, is part of keeping your ear to the ground.

**KEEP YOUR PRIORITIES RIGHT**

Of course, completing your Faith Promise is a matter of priorities, too. If World Evangelism is not your foremost pursuit in life, often monies God supplies and opportunities He provides for earnings are too easily squandered on

# THE WORLD'S MOST EXCITING PARTNERSHIP!

A short time ago, you responded to the Holy Spirit's leading to enlist as a Faith Promise Partner. God bless you for your obedience to the Lord's leading and congratulations on your new venture of faith. This same kind of faith and commitment will result in your goal fulfilled.

Here are some suggestions for Faith Promise Partners to help you achieve your individual and church Faith Promise goal.

1. Pray regularly for God's Financial Supply, either through bringing unexpected funds to yo or by giving you an Idea for Income.

2. Read the Labels Right on funds that come to you. Sometimes God's supply comes through in an increase in wages, gifts, bonus of some kind. Be alert to His supply.

3. Work your Idea for Income. God will use the industry of your hands for World Evangelism. One man raised steer. A woman raised African violets. They gave the profits for missions.

4. Give your money immediately as God supplies it. In this way, your collective monthly church goal will be met. God is faithful! And if your portion should not come in – keep praying – trusting – and looking! It might be delayed, but it will come. Someone else will, no doubt, have an extra supply to make up for those times your supply doesn't come in.

5. Give your Faith Promise through your Local Church.

6. Consult with your Pastor for prayer when your Faith Promise is in trouble. "If two of you shall agree…it shall be done." When a "trial of your faith" comes, remember it's only the doorway to a miracle. Keep trusting!

7. Don't "cheat" on your tithe. The tithe belongs to the local church for local church needs and ministries: "Bring ye the tithe into the storehouse…that there may be meat (necessary resources) in min house." (Mal. 3:10). Your Faith Promise is additional to your tithe – the result of a Faith venture you enter with God to believe Him to supply for World Missions a sum of money He put on your heart during the Missions Convention. If you violate this principle, it will bring untold injury, not only to your local church, but to World Missions, as well. It's best not to give to Missions at all, if you must take the tithe to do it! God's Pattern of doing things always works out best!

8. Share your Testimony. When God provides your Faith Promise in an unusual way, share it with your church. The church will be encouraged; their faith inspired to trust God more. In this way, we can spread the blessing far and wide: God is true to His Word. He IS faithful!

---

*"WHY SHOULD ANYONE HEAR THE GOSPEL TWICE WHEN SO MANY HAVE NOT HEARD IT ONCE?"*

# FIRST THINGS
# FOR
# FAITH PROMISE
# PARTNERS

---

**REGARDLESS** OF YOUR

AGE,

GENDER,

RACE,

INCOME,

EDUCATION,

STATUS, OR

STATION IN LIFE......

**OUR GOD CAN SUPPLY FOR MISSIONS**

## "MONIES
## YOU DON'T HAVE,
## FROM SOURCES YOU
## DON'T KNOW ABOUT"

# FAITH PROMISE

*How You Can Give to Missions, Money You Don't Have From Sources You Don't Know About*

## The Key

**Get a Word from God.** Ask **Him** what you should trust Him to provide through you for missions.
**God's Promise to You is *NOT According to Money you have...***
*In your pocket, Your budget, In your bank account Not Your Tithe...*
*BUT* what He will supply *beyond* that!

**No One Can Tell *YOU* What To Give.**
It is a Personal Faith Adventure.
It's Different for Everyone.

**Give the Lord Opportunity to Make a Promise to You.**

*"According to your faith be it unto you." Matthew 9:29*

## Your Response

**Record Your Faith Promise** *on a Faith Promise card*
This record is a "Proof" of Your Promise to God
It is Completely Confidential and will NOT be published
It will NOT be demanded of you by the church.
If the money is not being forthcoming, just "Tell it to the Lord!"

*Actively Trust God for your Faith Promise.*

*Be on the "Look-out" for God's provision.*

*Read the Labels Right!* As you get the money, *keep your word.*

Give it!

*According to your faith be it unto you" Matthew 9:29*

---

# FAITH PROMISE

*How You Can Give to Missions, Money You Don't Have From Sources You Don't Know About*

## The Key

**Get a Word from God.** Ask **Him** what you should trust Him to provide through you for missions.
**God's Promise to You is *NOT According to Money you have...***
*In your pocket, Your budget, In your bank account Not Your Tithe...*
*BUT* what He will supply *beyond* that!

**No One Can Tell *YOU* What To Give.**
It is a Personal Faith Adventure.
It's Different for Everyone.

**Give the Lord Opportunity to Make a Promise to You.**

*"According to your faith be it unto you." Matthew 9:29*

## Your Response

**Record Your Faith Promise** *on a Faith Promise Card*
This record is a "Proof" of Your Promise to God
It is Completely Confidential and will NOT be published
It will NOT be demanded of you by the church.
If the money is not being forthcoming, just "Tell it to the Lord!"

*Actively Trust God for your Faith Promise.*

*Be on the "Look-out" for God's provision.*

*Read the Labels Right!* As money comes in, *keep your word!*

Give it!

*According to your faith be it unto you" Matthew 9:29*

# My Faith Promise

## TO HELP REAP THE HARVEST

I will trust the Lord to supply the amount of money I believe He has put in my heart and will faithfully give it for missions through my local church.

Monthly Amount $_____   X 12 =   Annual Amount  $_____

NAME_____

ADDRESS_____

CITY/STATE/ZIP_____

EMAIL_____ PHONE_____

*"...I WILL SHOW YOU MY FAITH BY MY WORKS"  -James 2:18*

← CUT ALONG THIS LINE

### MY FAITH PROMISE REMINDER

I recorded a
Faith Promise total of

$_____

for this year.
I will pray and trust
the Lord to provide
this amount; and
faithfully give it for
missions as the Lord
supplies it through
usual or unexpected
sources.

## DO I REALLY BELIEVE QUICKIE SELF-QUIZ

**T   F**

___  ___  People are lost without Christ

___  ___  Lost people spend eternity separated from God

___  ___  Lost people cannot save themselves

___  ___  The Lost must hear the Gospel

___  ___  They cannot hear without a preacher

___  ___  Salvation is free but it costs to proclaim it

___  ___  God owns everything

___  ___  The money I have I only manage for God

___  ___  The salvation of a person is the most important thing

___  ___  My monies are placed best when placed in missions

___  ___  God's managers respect that priority &  it shows my love

___  ___  Even if I'm poor, I'm better off than 2/3rds of the world

___  ___  There's really no reason I cannot make a Faith Promise

___  ___  Faith & Compassion make possible the Impossible

___  ___  God is faithful & will provide my Faith Promise

___  ___  If my Faith Promise isn't completed, I explain only to God

___  ___  The Faith Promise I now make will result in souls saved

*" GOD WILL PROVIDE FOR MISSIONS,*
*MONEY I DON'T HAVE,*
*FROM SOURCES,*
*I DON'T KNOW ABOUT"*

## FAITH PROMISE POINTERS

A Faith Promise Card should be in the hands of each person.  Children also should be given the opportunity to register a personal Faith Promise.  Even though they might register a small amount, they will grow up with sensitivity to their responsibility in missions and develop into substantial givers as young people and adults.

Duplicate enough Cards to include in a pre-Ingathering mailing to each person and make sure there are plenty to provide each person during the Sunday Morning Ingathering service.

Instruct the people to determine how much they believe the Lord wants them to trust Him to provide through them for missions each month and write that amount on their Faith Promise Card.  Then have them multiply that amount by 12 and write that amount on their Card.  This will make it easier for the person who reads the annual amount of each Card publically during the Ingathering Service.  (Only the amount is read; not the identity of the person on the Card.)  Pause for a subtotal periodically & report the total for the inspiration of the people & display it on your Missions Thermometer.  It can be a powerfully exciting time!  The total you register will be the goal for the year for your congregation.

# 5. *Sample Letters to Challenge Faith Partners*

## *First Christian Assembly*

000 Second Avenue
Any City, OH 00000

Guy BonGiovanni, D. Min.
Interim Pastor

**"Why should anyone hear the Gospel _twice_**
**When so many have not heard it once?"**

Dear Friend:

That statement really impacted my life when I first heard it several years ago. Like most people I had been too casual about missions. It was hard for me to believe there still might be people, other than primitive tribesmen, who hadn't heard about Jesus at least once.

*But I got a shocking wake-up call* one day from my friend Angelo. I was showing him one of my oil paintings depicting the Rapture of the church. As I explained what it was all about, he looked at me in disbelief and said, "I never heard that before." And he lived just a few blocks from me, not in the Amazon jungle!

**There are millions around the world who yet haven't heard the Gospel just once!**
**And there are millions more who need to be "discipled" in the Faith.**

That's why so many dedicated men and women, young people like our own James Sabella and Greg Mundas leave friends and family. *Their passion to tell people about Jesus drives them*, in spite of the cost' like the Giordanos who when we saw them off in New York's harbor on a freighter to Paraguay, Mrs. Giordano knew *she would never again see her mother on this earth*! I don't know how that makes you feel, but it sure humbles me!

Whether or not you are a member or just a friend of First Christian Assembly, I have no doubt *you have a heart for missions, too*. And I urge you to share with us in our exciting Missions Convention over the next few weeks. Colorful banners, posters, flags and an enthusiastic congregation will greet you. On the last Sunday, ushers dressed in colorful costumes will gather the Faith Promises. Of course the big barometer also is ready for action.

**It will be exciting to see how far our faith will take us.**

I've enclosed a Faith Promise card for you because *I don't want you to miss out in this* special opportunity to demonstrate with others your level of dedication and faith. All of us can't do what the Giordanos did, but each of us can serve with our giving. Please record the amount you will trust the Lord to supply on the enclosed Faith Promise Card. Bring it to the church on "Faith Promise Sunday," or mail it if you cannot come. When we add it all up we will see exactly what will be our *Missions goal is for the year – and the level of our faith*. The testimonials of God's miraculous supply throughout the year will bless us!

*One of the most frequent questions I'm asked* is, "Brother BonGiovanni, how much should my Faith Promise be?" As you know the Faith Promise is a very personal thing so I can't tell anyone how much to give. But I do remind them King David set a good example for us when he said, "I will not offer to the Lord what costs me nothing;" then I suggest one carefully reviews his budget to see what he can afford to give for missions *from his budget*. Then **ask the Lord** to show you *how much **He** would like you to trust Him to provide for Missions* above that amount over the next 12 months. That's what's given *from his faith.* Add the two amounts together and you have your personal Faith Promise goal.

**It will amaze you how the Lord will bring you for missions money you don't have from sources you don't even know about**.

*What an adventure of faith that will be!* Please understand, this is a matter between you and the Lord. **It is NOT a pledge! No one will press you for it.** You only will be asked to trust the Lord for it – and we will help you pray that the Lord will do the miracle for you when it's needed. There are literally thousands of testimonials of people who have seen miracles like this; and *you will be no exception.*

If you believe there is a Heaven to gain and a Hell to shun; and that Jesus is the Answer; then help us do all we can to go "Everywhere" and reach everyone with the Gospel while we yet have time.

Blessings on you, dear Friend. We're so pleased to have you as a partner in the Gospel.

**Sincerely,**
***"In Pursuit of Excellence,"***


**Guy BonGiovanni, D. Min.**


P. S.   Please be in prayer, especially during these important weeks!  "Except the Lord build the house, they labor in vain who build it."


Encl.:   Faith Promise Card


# NOTE:   THIS SAMPLE LETTER SHOULD BE TAILORED TO FIT YOUR OWN TIME-FRAME AND CONGREGATION

## 5. SAMPLE LETTERS TO CHALLENGE FAITH PROMISE PARTNERS

*[For Children & Young People]*

## *"Everywhere" Starts with me!*

**Hey, my young friend!**

If I had to believe some people, I'd have to believe my young friends don't have a heart for hurting people; and they don't want to help others.

***But I don't believe it!***

I'm convinced children and young people are <u>*just as deeply concerned*</u> as adults – sometimes even more. That's why I'm sending you this special letter and the enclosed Faith Promise card. I know hundreds of young people and children just like you who trust the Lord for money they don't have, so they can give to help other children, young people and adults that really are hurting. And ***I just believe you want to help, too.***

I know if you ask the Lord to help you know how much you should give for missions over the next 12 months, <u>He will help you know</u>. He can give you ideas how to earn it, or get it to you in amazing ways. I know! I've seen it happen in <u>*my daughters when they were just children*</u> and then teen agers.

***Help me prove*** that children and young people can be just as sensitive as adults about helping others. Talk to the Lord in your own way about <u>how much</u> <u>He wants you to trust Him to provide</u> through you. Then write it on the Faith Promise card and bring it to church on Faith Promise Sunday. I won't be reading people's names, but ***I will be so proud*** to read the amount <u>you write</u> on your card and add it to the total church goal ***because it says, "I care!"***

It will be an exciting time! I want you to be part of it.

Blessings on you, my young friend.

Sincerely,
"In Pursuit of Excellence,"

*Guy BonGiovanni, D. Min.*
Interim Pastor

TAILOR TO YOUR OWN CHURCH NEEDS !!!

# 6. Powerful Statements & Slogans That Energize Missions

► "Why should anyone hear the Gospel twice before everyone has heard it once?"
 –  Dr. Oswald J. Smith

► "Christ accepted makes you a Christian; Christ obeyed makes you a missionary" –Anon

► "Let my heart be broken by the things that break the heart of God"
 –Bob Pierce, founder of World Vision

► "It is as necessary for men to hear the Gospel as it was for Christ to die" – Anon

► "Christ alone can save the world; Christ cannot save the world alone" –Anon

► "This generation of Christians is responsible for this generation of souls on the earth" –Keith Green

► "Millions dying there have never heard; millions living here have never cared" –Anon

► "If I found a cure for cancer, wouldn't it be inconceivable to hide it from the rest of mankind?  How much more inconceivable to keep silent the cure from the eternal wages of sin!"
 –Dave Davidson

► "There is nothing in the world or the Church –except the church's disobedience – to render the evangelization of the world in this generation an impossibility." –Robert Speer

► "Expect great things from God; attempt great things for God" –William Carey, father of modern missions

► "If God calls you to be a missionary, don't stoop to be a king." Jordan Groom

► "We died before we came here," was the succinct response James Calvert gave the ship's captain, who  urged  him and his team to return home because the cannibals of the Fiji Islands would kill them – "you will lose your lives!" -Hudson Taylor

► "God's work done in God's way will never lack God's supply" –Hudson Taylor

► "The spirit of Christ is the spirit of missions.  The nearer we get to Him, the more intensely missionary we become." – Henry Martyn

► "The Great Commission is not an option to be considered; it is a command to be obeyed"
 –Hudson Taylor

► "Some wish to live within the sound of a chapel bell; I wish to run a rescue mission within a yard of hell." – C.T. Studd

# The Faith Promise Concept...

# Do It !

1. Get a Personal word FROM God

2. Give your word TO God

3. ACTIVELY TRUST God to supply it

4. LOOK for it

5. GIVE it !

# Sermon Outlines
## on the
## Faith Promise

# The Faith Promise

**INTRO:**

**A.** **Until early 60s I had no personal program for Involvement in Missions**
1. As an Individual: gave to missions
2. As Pastor: scheduled Missionaries.
3. I did all the right & expected things.
4. Then realized I had no Personal Program. I was very uncomfortable, began to seek the Lord.

**B.** **Finally, I made a Discovery that was Destined to Revolutionize my Personal life & Denomination**
1. My Personal Giving increased dramatically
2. Our Local Church: giving to Missions increased by 530 %
3. Later, Introduced it to Denomination - increased by 700%
4. Personally counted out in Missions Conventions at least $1 million

**C.** **That Discovery is Called a Faith Promise:**
1. The F.P. first introduced to church by Dr. A.B.Simpson;
   promoted by Dr. O.J. Smith of-Toronto, Canada)
   (Smith believed it so strongly, told me, no one could serve on his eldership Board of 200 if they didn't register a F.P.)
2. Very Basically: F.P. is a Record of an Amount of Money one Sincerely Believes God wants him to Trust God to Supply for Mission through him.
3. The Exciting Fact is that Thru the F.P., *God can provide for Missions, Money you don't Have, From Sources You Don't Know About!*

**D.** **Success in the Lord's Work Depends on 4 Things:**
1. Call of God              (to Motivate it);
2. Commission of God        (to Focus Efforts)
3. Charismata of Spirit     (to Accomplish it);
4. CASH                     (to Pay bills for it !!)
(Absence of any one of these Cripples. Fact is: It Takes Money to do God's Work!)

From what I can see,

**I.** **THE BIBLE PATTERN FOR FINANCING GOD'S WORK INCLUDES 3 Streams of Income:**

**A.** **Tithes & Offerings**               (Covenant of Blessing): Based on Mal.3:10
      *Provides for Internal Operation* & (Capital Expenditures: i.e. buildings, etcs.)

**B.** **Communion (Eucharist) Offering:**
      *Provides for Benevolence* Described by Early Church.Fathers &
      hinted at in Matt. 5:23,24: "leave thy gift at the altar…"

**C.** **Faith Promise:** (No "Proof Text", a "Theological Construct" cf. "Trinity")
      *Provides for World Missions*      *Based on Combination of Scriptures:*
      Jhn.15:7 "If my words abide in you…ask what ye will & it shall be done unto you."
      2 Cor.8:3,4 (Macedonians gave "to the limit of their resources, & then even beyond their power"
      Birthed in Compassion

D.    When these are in Place, Should be Enough Money to accomplish what God Expects from Church

## II.    *THE BASIC INGREDIENTS IN THE FAITH PROMISE:*

**A.    A Word From the Lord:** F.P. is Based on What One Believes God has told him to Give
(John. 15:7 "If my words abide in you...ask what ye will & it shall be done"

   1.    *The Wisdom of the Lord is Seen in that the F.P.:*
      a.    is <u>Not Based on one's Economic Condition</u> (Children; Sr. Citizen.; students, Retirees- everyone can tap into God's Supply
      b.    is <u>Not Based on one's Budget or Bank Acct.</u> (O.J.Smith used to say "Just tell your hand to write check" if it's based on one's bank account.

   2.    *Your Question will Be: "Lord, How much do YOU want me to Trust you to Supply for Mission thru me?"*

   3.    *Three Considerations in the Word of the Lord to You:*
      a.    Might Require a **Budget Adjustment:** (Won't say like Compolo, "If you have a BMW repent," but will suggest *reevaluate* your values/priorities.
      b.    Might come with an "**Idea for Income:**" (Lady raised African Violets - supported Native Evangelists; Man raised a steer - became "Steer, Inc."; Garage Sale, etc.)
         1)    God Expects us to be Entrepreneurs:  We should Generate as much as we can so we can give more
            (Parable of Talents:  Matt. 25:14-29 (5 & 2 talents- 100% return, 1 talent- loss!)
            Get into business!  Note: God didn't give the widow "buckets of Money," only opportunity!
      c.    Might Require a **Creative Miracle:** (Julie's Inheritance: $1m = 2 gold coins)

**B.    An Action of Faith:**
   1.    **(Faith is a virtue given to every person** (Rom.12: "dealt to every man a <u>measure</u> of faith" (Matt. 8: "little" & "great") Need it when challenged; not for a sure thing)
      *Needed When One Faces:*
      a.    <u>Impossible</u>:     (Cross River Jordan)
      b.    <u>Irrational</u>:     (Widow challenged to give Prophet last meal she had; Joshua to walk around Jericho to capture the city.)
      c.    <u>Invisible God</u>: (When there is No Visible source of help) i.e.-Moses-"endured, as seeing him who is invisible"

   2.    **Three Actions of Faith You Must Take for Faith Promise:**
      a.    ***Step #1:*** Get Your Word from the Lord: *That's HIS Promise to You!* (Comes by Budget Analysis ***Plus;*** Revelation of amount in your spirit; or as an Idea for Income)
      b.    ***Step #2:*** Record That Word: (F.P.):     *That's YOUR Promise to God!*
      c.    ***Step #3:*** Take Action on Basis of His Word to You:
         1)    WORK your "Idea for Income"
         2)    PRAY for Release of Resources
         3)    GIVE Money as it Comes In

C. **Faith Promise Elevates Nature of Giving:** Giving becomes an Expression of one's Relationship w/God! Intimacy.
   1. Lifts Giving <u>out of Realm of Impulsive Response</u> to emotional stories
   2. Lifts Giving <u>into Realm of Spiritual Wisdom</u> (Intelligent Giving)
   3. Don't give because of Feeling, Fear, Coercion, Peer Pressure
      It's as though **the Lord** says - "I want to bless the people of Mexico. But we need CASH for the Laborers there. Do you think you can Partner with Me in this adventure of faith.
      **You Ask**: How much, Lord? He helps you understand: $400.
      **You Respond**, "Yes, Lord, I'll trust you."
      **Then** you pray, trust, watch for it to come in, or for special opportunities to earn it.

**III.** *BELIEVERS IN THE FAITH PROMISE:* <u>*GET A WORD FROM GOD & RECORD IT AS AN EXPRESSION OF THEIR FAITH*</u>

   A. **How Much Shall I Trust God For?** A <u>*Personal*</u> Matter: Your <u>*personal*</u> Venture of Faith
      1. A F. P. is What YOU believe God wants YOU to Trust Him to Supply for Missions thru YOU!
      2. Remember: Hebrews 5:14 "learned to discern…by reason of use" -experience
         a. We grow in our Ability to Discern God's Voice: when I was a child act as a child
         b. Faith is a Virtue that Grows w/Use: "Lord, Increase my faith"; "go from faith to faith"
            Exercise Wisdom. Avoid Extreamism – i.e.-believe for a Million!
   B. **How Does God Talk to Us?** (Not usually by an Audible Voice)
      a. Often: Thoughts fill one's mind; you feel comfortable with it
      b. An Inner impression/conviction; dreams; a "business" analysis
   C. **Three Final Thoughts:**
      1. The F.P. is <u>NOT a Pledge</u>. A pledge is a Legal Document that can be demanded
      2. There Might be <u>a Trial of Faith</u>: (Tell Pastor about it for Prayer… i.e. Mrs. "P" regestered $300 based on Teaching job, but 2M applicants in NYC ahead of her. She got the job!)
      3. <u>Read the Labels Right:</u> when Money comes in, give it !

*CONCL.*

A. We live in a World of Overwhelming Need:

B. How Can we Meet It? With Resources in God. We must do as He Says!

**"God can Provide for Mission <u>*Through You:*</u>
Monies You Don't Have,
From Sources You Don't Know About."**

"And this gospel of the kingdom shall be preached
in all the world for a witness unto all nations:
and then shall the end come" Matt.24:14

# "Possibility Giving"

"God hath dealt to every man a measure of faith" Rom. 12:3
"According to your faith be it unto you" Matt. 9:29

## I.  THE FAITH PROMISE AS THE BIBLICAL PATTERN

A. The Covenant Tithe:       For Local Concerns
B. The Special Offerings:    For Occasional Special Needs
   1. Charity:
   2. Emergencies:
   3. Capital Expenditures:
C. The Faith Promise:        For World Missions
   1. Monies you Don't Have
   2. Sources you Don't Know About
   3. Conditioned by one's assets/income vs. Needs

## II.  THE FAITH PROMISE AS A POSSIBILITY FOR YOU

A. A Proven Method
B. Possibility Giving is for You
   1. You have a Unique Authority Base        John 1:12
   2. You have the same Equipment as Others   Romans 12
   3. You have an Unusual Guidance System     Romans 8:14
   4. You don't need a Miracle for Everything Eccl. 9:10
   5. You can Expect a Miracle if it is Needed  Matt.18:24-27

## III.  THE FAITH PROMISE AS A PROCEDURE

A. **Get a word from God.** What is the Amount He is leading you to trust Him to supply for Missions through you over the next year?

B. **Give Your Word to God.** Register it in a Faith Promise

**CONCL.**

A. The Urgency of World Need           Matt. 9:35-38

B. The Ugliness of Ignoring World Need  Matt. 25: 31-46

SERMON OUTLINES    #2a

# Possibility Giving (Expanded)

Intro:  Dr. Falkenburg, Dir. of NY Bible Society gave Gospel to Tribal Chief in India
   Indian Chief, weeping convulsivly:  " I didn't know God had a Son,
               "I didn't know He died for us.
               "Why didn't someone tell us??
   He represents millions who have not heard.
   ***Challenge*: "Why should anyone hear Gospel twice**
       **when millions have not heard it once?"**
   Requires two (2) things:
    1. Love
    2. Giving to meet the need.
   Two Observations:
    1. You can be inspired with Promises of God for Prosperity.
      Christian  knows it can be used for missions/needy.
     You think:  "I wish I could have/give like that"
     Scripture Encourages:"Give & it shall be given unto you, pressed down, shaken
      together, running over will men give unto thy bosom."
    2. You can be inspired  with  the Giving Record/testimony of
     another.  It Creates a desire in your heart.
     You think: "I wish I could be like that"

**FACT IS**:  It is Possible! "Yes you can!"
     You may need to RECYCLE your mind to a posture of Possibility
     "I Can"   If can't reach that, consider: "I might be ABLE to" Move off:" I can't"

**SEVERAL REASONS FOR IT**:
  1.  You Are God's Child: Have power through Position. No longer aliens from God (Eph.2)
    "Come Boldly to God's Throne" as His Children & Servants

  2.  You Have Same Equipment as Others –Inside you!
    "Unto each is given a measure of faith"- little/great   Romans 12
    (Might be Rusty or "out of line" –but it's there)
    (Possibility: Faith machinery needs attention. lubrication with Word, Anointing, and
     Compassion will ignite vision)

  3.  You Have an Unusual Guidance System.   Romans 8:14
    "led by the Spirit" "hear his voice"
    Must learn to use it thru Trial & Error: "elders by reason of use learned to discern
    between right/wrong"       Hebrews 5:14

  4.  Everything that's Good that you Can Do, Doesn't take a Miracle.
    Frequently only common sense is direction enough.
    (You see a need – you have a dollar –give it!)
    "That which thy hand findeth to do," do it...'   Eccl. 9:10

  5.  God will bring you Beyond Yourself, if necessary
    He will do a miracle, if necessary.   Matthew 19:26

SERMON OUTLINE        3

Hebrews 11:6; Matt. 9:29
Matt. 17: 24-27

# Creative Faith

### "How to Turn your Faith into Cash"

**INTRO:**

    A.    Creedal Faith involves Basic Doctrines: i.e. Apostles' Creed

    B.    Creative Faith involves Activated / Exercised Faith

    C.    Lesson Base: Peter's discovery of Tribute Money in a fish's mouth

## I.   THE **MARKINGS** OF THE MIRACLE MONEY:
(God knows where the Money is for your Faith Promise as he knew where the Tribute Money was)

Notice His accuracy in Marking where the fish were located:
A.    Luke 5: 1-7        "a great multitude of fish"

B.    John 21: 1-11      "full of great fish"

## II.  THE **MYSTIQUE** OF THE MIRACLE SUPPLY:
(God might work "Outside the box" for your Faith Promise)

    A.    From <u>Unusual</u> Sources: v.27    The "sea" is not where you store your money.

    B.    From <u>Unexpected</u> Sources: v.27 Most people would be startled to find money in a fish's mouth.

## III.  THE **MANDATE** REQUIRED FOR THE MIRACLE SUPPLY:
(Getting a Word from God is Key to your Faith Promise: "go to the sea...")

    A.    Creative Faith is Obedience to the Word the Lord gives you. Luke 5:5

    B.    The pivotal word in negative circumstances is: "nevertheless" v.5

## IV.  THE **MUNIFICENCE** OF THE MIRACLE SUPPLY:
(God's Supply for Faith Promises is "Enough, PLUS.")

    A.    A Kingdom Principle: "pressed down and running over." Luke 6:38

    B.    The Response to Creative Faith: "their net broke"      Luke 5:6

**"You can partner with God in missions
Regardless of age, gender and economic status"**

*"According to your faith be it unto you"*-Jesus Matt. 9:29

# Notes

www.ingramcontent.com/pod-product-compliance
Lightning Source LLC
Chambersburg PA
CBHW081151040426
42445CB00015B/1845